BABY SHOWER GUEST BOOK

THIS BOOK BELONGS TO..

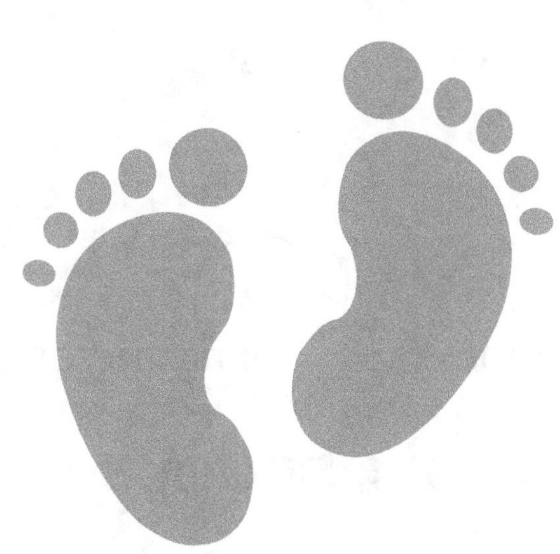

OLIVIA BROOKS

Name

Relationship to the parents/baby

Wishes for the parents

Wishes for the baby

My best advice for parents

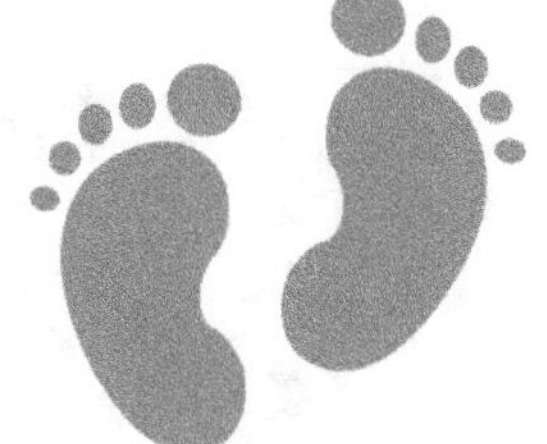

Name

Relationship to the parents/baby

Wishes for the parents

Wishes for the baby

My best advice for parents

Name

Relationship to the parents/baby

Wishes for the parents

Wishes for the baby

My best advice for parents

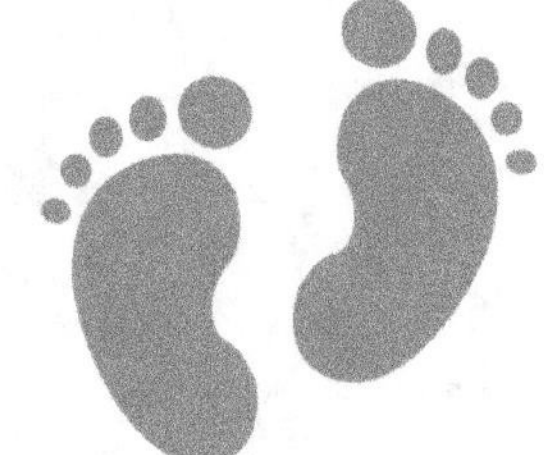

Name

Relationship to the parents/baby

Wishes for the parents

Wishes for the baby

My best advice for parents

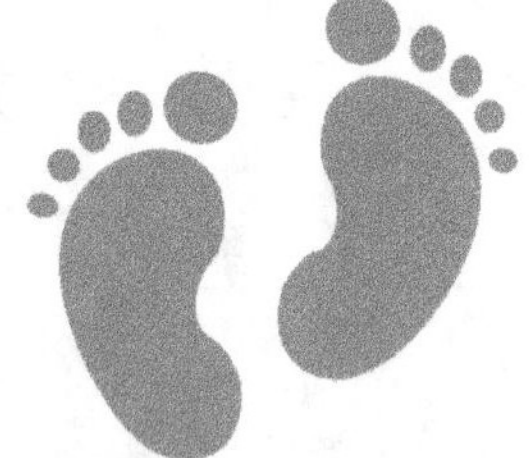

Name

Relationship to the parents/baby

Wishes for the parents

Wishes for the baby

My best advice for parents

Name

Relationship to the parents/baby

Wishes for the parents

Wishes for the baby

My best advice for parents

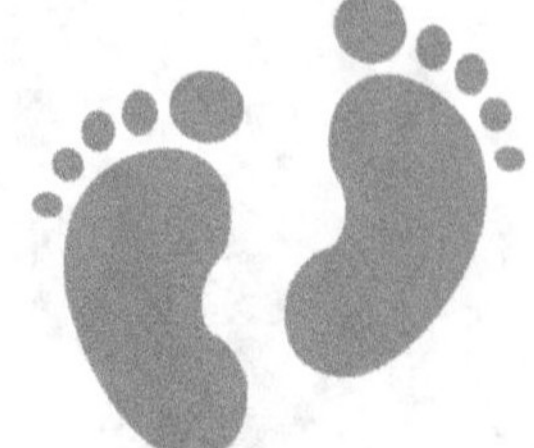

Name

Relationship to the parents/baby

Wishes for the parents

Wishes for the baby

My best advice for parents

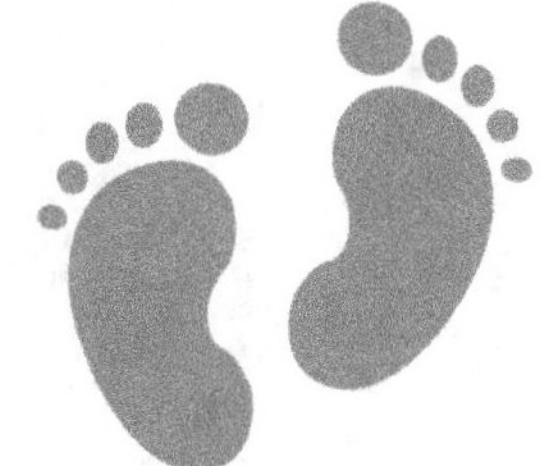

Name

Relationship to the parents/baby

Wishes for the parents

Wishes for the baby

My best advice for parents

Name

Relationship to the parents/baby

Wishes for the parents

Wishes for the baby

My best advice for parents

Name

Relationship to the parents/baby

Wishes for the parents

Wishes for the baby

My best advice for parents

Name

Relationship to the parents/baby

Wishes for the parents

Wishes for the baby

My best advice for parents

Name

Relationship to the parents/baby

Wishes for the parents

Wishes for the baby

My best advice for parents

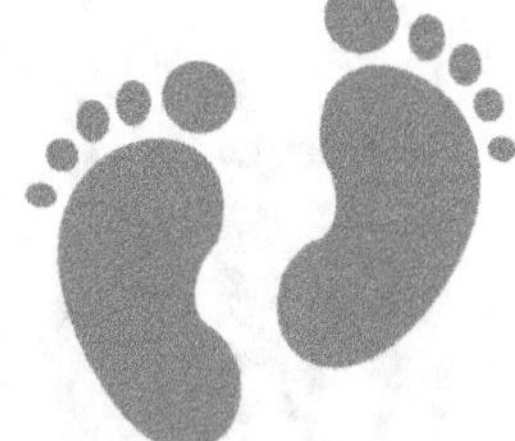

Name

Relationship to the parents/baby

Wishes for the parents

Wishes for the baby

My best advice for parents

Name

Relationship to the parents/baby

Wishes for the parents

Wishes for the baby

My best advice for parents

Name

Relationship to the parents/baby

Wishes for the parents

Wishes for the baby

My best advice for parents

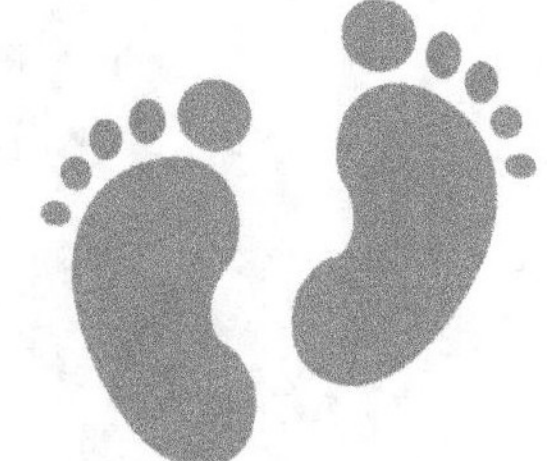

Name

Relationship to the parents/baby

Wishes for the parents

Wishes for the baby

My best advice for parents

Name

- -

Relationship to the parents/baby

Wishes for the parents

- -

- -

- -

- -

Wishes for the baby

- -

- -

- -

My best advice for parents

- -

- -

- -

Name

Relationship to the parents/baby

Wishes for the parents

Wishes for the baby

My best advice for parents

Name

Relationship to the parents/baby
Wishes for the parents

Wishes for the baby

My best advice for parents

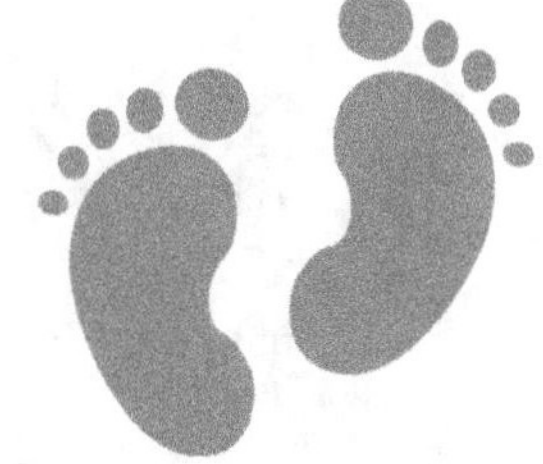

Name

Relationship to the parents/baby

Wishes for the parents

Wishes for the baby

My best advice for parents

Name

Relationship to the parents/baby

Wishes for the parents

Wishes for the baby

My best advice for parents

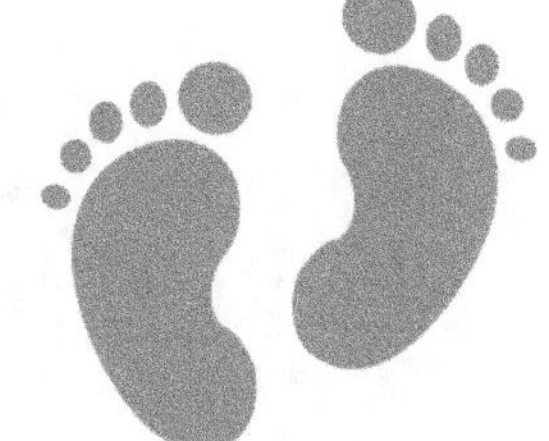

Name

Relationship to the parents/baby

Wishes for the parents

Wishes for the baby

My best advice for parents

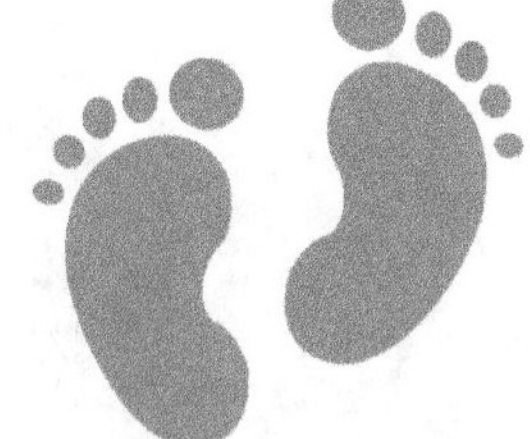

Name

Relationship to the parents/baby

Wishes for the parents

Wishes for the baby

My best advice for parents

Name

Relationship to the parents/baby

Wishes for the parents

Wishes for the baby

My best advice for parents

Name

Relationship to the parents/baby

Wishes for the parents

Wishes for the baby

My best advice for parents

  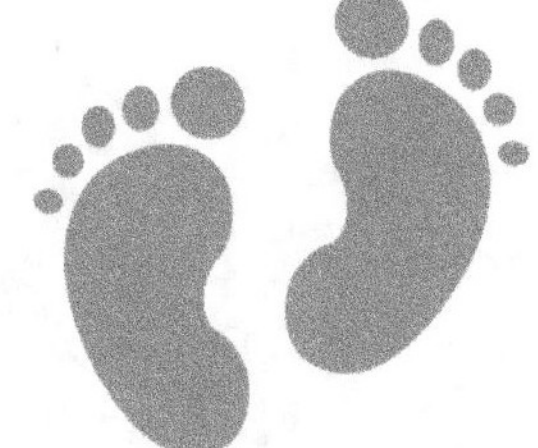  

Name

Relationship to the parents/baby

Wishes for the parents

Wishes for the baby

My best advice for parents

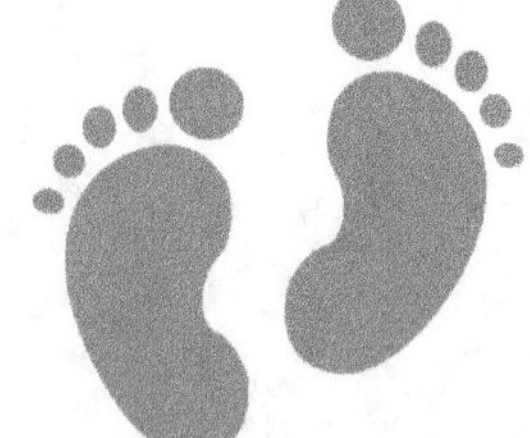

Name

Relationship to the parents/baby
Wishes for the parents

Wishes for the baby

My best advice for parents

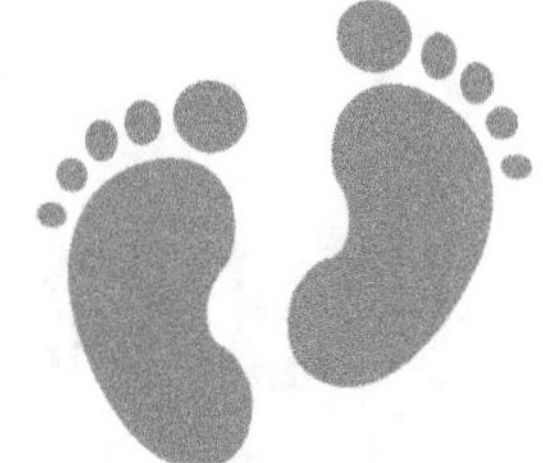

Name

Relationship to the parents/baby

Wishes for the parents

Wishes for the baby

My best advice for parents

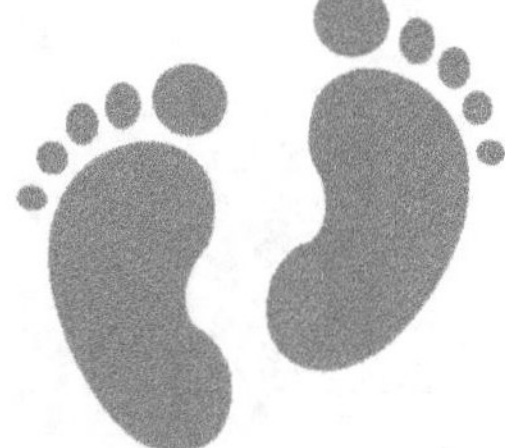

Name

Relationship to the parents/baby

Wishes for the parents

Wishes for the baby

My best advice for parents

Name

Relationship to the parents/baby

Wishes for the parents

Wishes for the baby

My best advice for parents

Name

Relationship to the parents/baby

Wishes for the parents

Wishes for the baby

My best advice for parents

Name

Relationship to the parents/baby

Wishes for the parents

Wishes for the baby

My best advice for parents

Name

Relationship to the parents/baby

Wishes for the parents

Wishes for the baby

My best advice for parents

Name

Relationship to the parents/baby

Wishes for the parents

Wishes for the baby

My best advice for parents

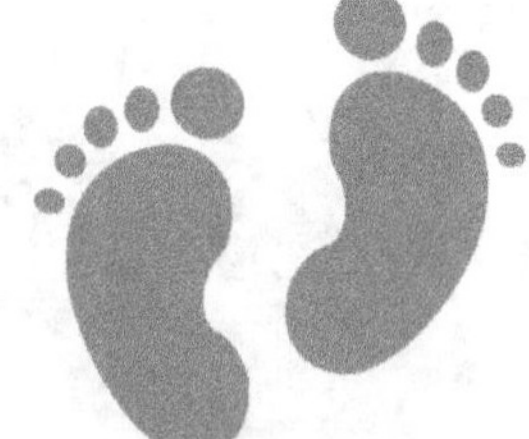

Name

Relationship to the parents/baby
Wishes for the parents

Wishes for the baby

My best advice for parents

Name

Relationship to the parents/baby

Wishes for the parents

Wishes for the baby

My best advice for parents

Name

Relationship to the parents/baby

Wishes for the parents

Wishes for the baby

My best advice for parents

Name

Relationship to the parents/baby

Wishes for the parents

Wishes for the baby

My best advice for parents

Name

Relationship to the parents/baby

Wishes for the parents

Wishes for the baby

My best advice for parents

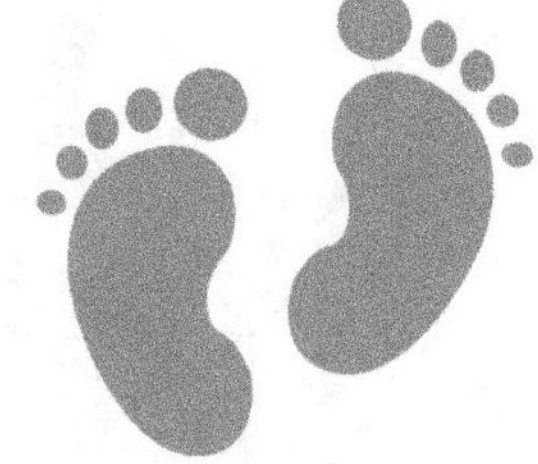

Name

Relationship to the parents/baby

Wishes for the parents

Wishes for the baby

My best advice for parents

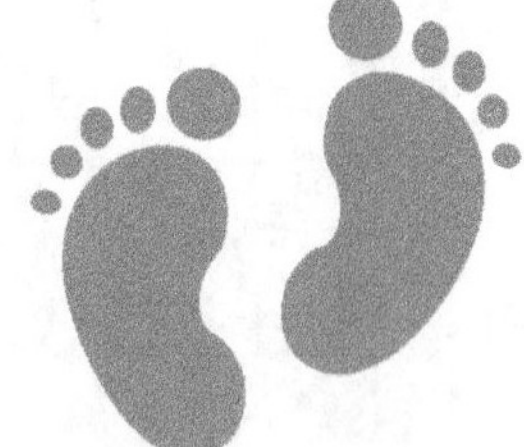

Name

Relationship to the parents/baby

Wishes for the parents

Wishes for the baby

My best advice for parents

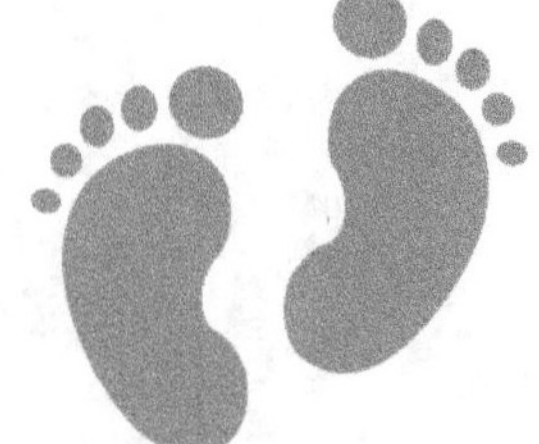

Name

Relationship to the parents/baby

Wishes for the parents

Wishes for the baby

My best advice for parents

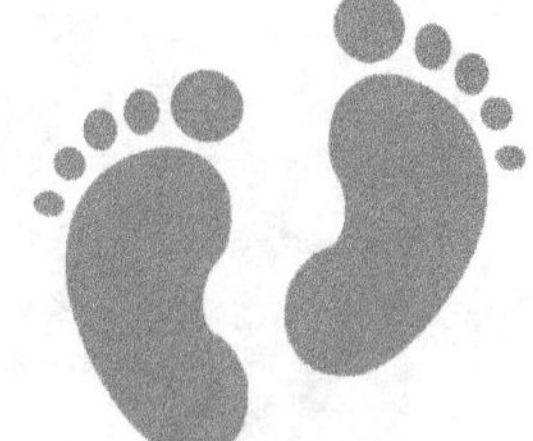

Name

Relationship to the parents/baby

Wishes for the parents

Wishes for the baby

My best advice for parents

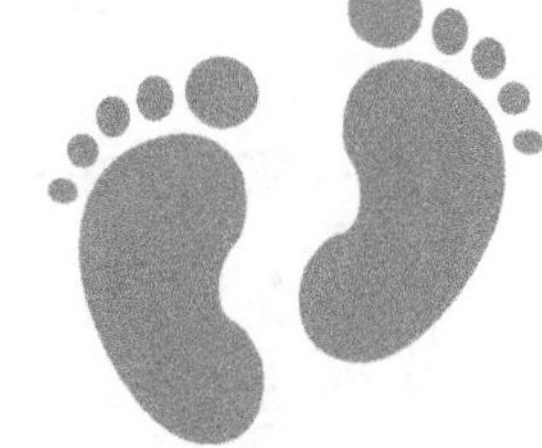

Name

Relationship to the parents/baby

Wishes for the parents

Wishes for the baby

My best advice for parents

Name

Relationship to the parents/baby

Wishes for the parents

Wishes for the baby

My best advice for parents

Name

Relationship to the parents/baby

Wishes for the parents

Wishes for the baby

My best advice for parents

Name

Relationship to the parents/baby

Wishes for the parents

Wishes for the baby

My best advice for parents

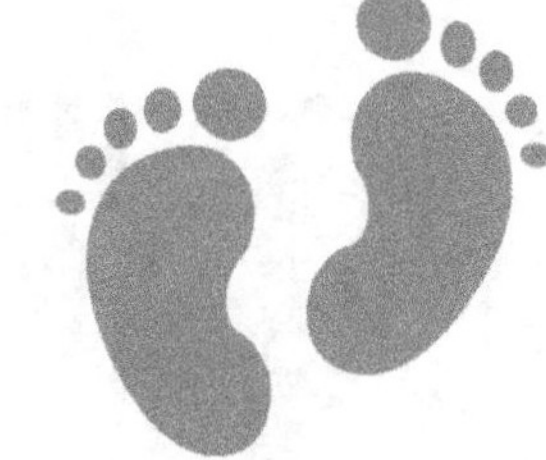

Name

Relationship to the parents/baby

Wishes for the parents

Wishes for the baby

My best advice for parents

Name

Relationship to the parents/baby
Wishes for the parents

Wishes for the baby

My best advice for parents

Name

Relationship to the parents/baby

Wishes for the parents

Wishes for the baby

My best advice for parents

Name

Relationship to the parents/baby

Wishes for the parents

Wishes for the baby

My best advice for parents

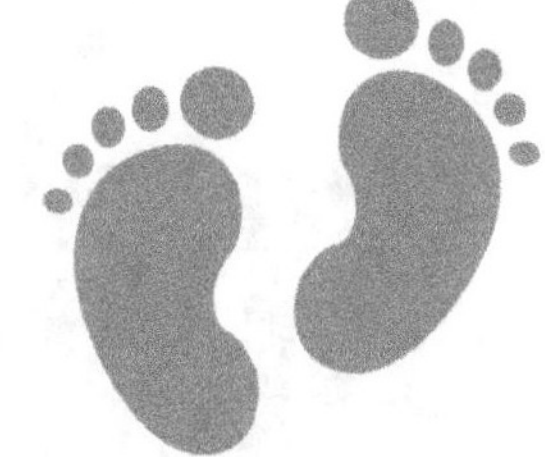

Name

Relationship to the parents/baby

Wishes for the parents

Wishes for the baby

My best advice for parents

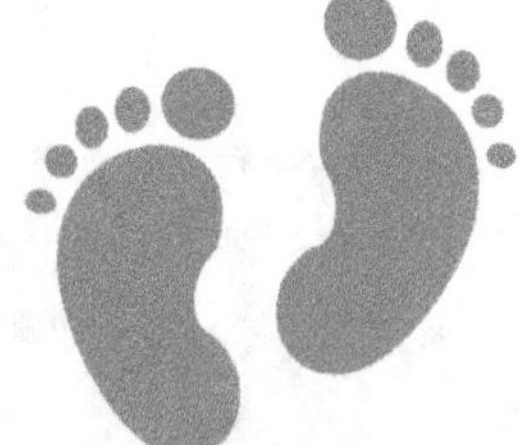

Name

Relationship to the parents/baby

Wishes for the parents

Wishes for the baby

My best advice for parents

Name

Relationship to the parents/baby

Wishes for the parents

Wishes for the baby

My best advice for parents

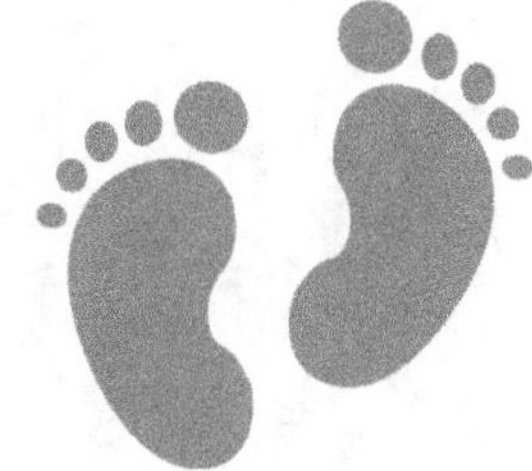

Name

Relationship to the parents/baby

Wishes for the parents

Wishes for the baby

My best advice for parents

Name

Relationship to the parents/baby

Wishes for the parents

Wishes for the baby

My best advice for parents

Name

Relationship to the parents/baby

Wishes for the parents

Wishes for the baby

My best advice for parents

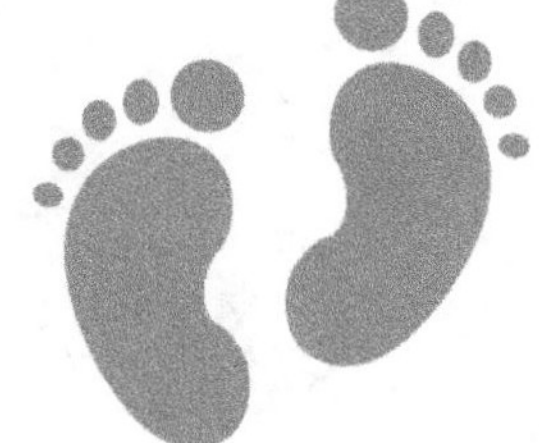

Name

Relationship to the parents/baby

Wishes for the parents

Wishes for the baby

My best advice for parents

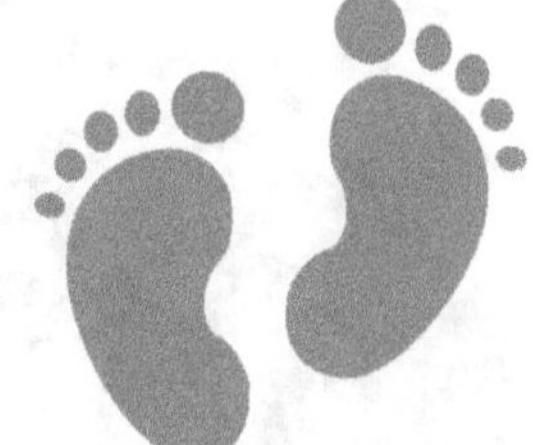

Name

Relationship to the parents/baby

Wishes for the parents

Wishes for the baby

My best advice for parents

Name

Relationship to the parents/baby

Wishes for the parents

Wishes for the baby

My best advice for parents

Name

Relationship to the parents/baby
Wishes for the parents

Wishes for the baby

My best advice for parents

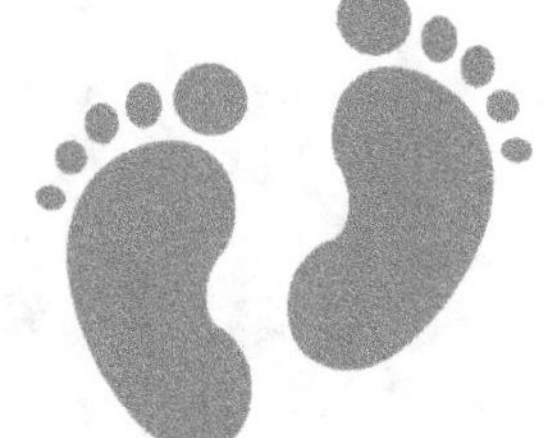

Name

Relationship to the parents/baby

Wishes for the parents

Wishes for the baby

My best advice for parents

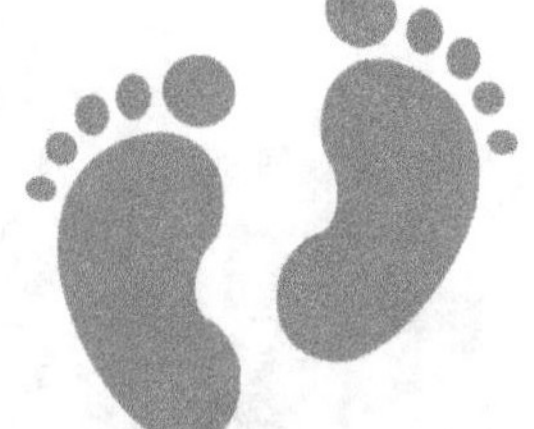

Name

Relationship to the parents/baby

Wishes for the parents

Wishes for the baby

My best advice for parents

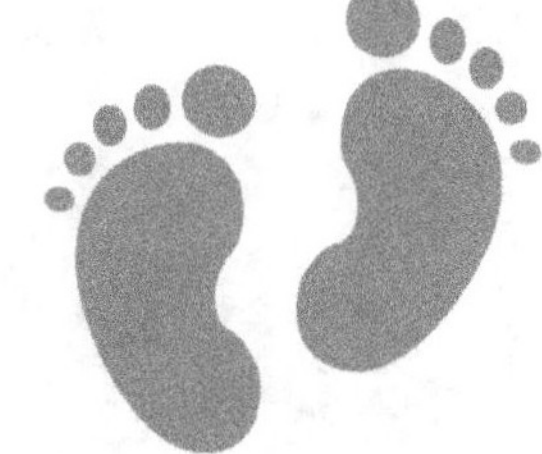

Name

Relationship to the parents/baby

Wishes for the parents

Wishes for the baby

My best advice for parents

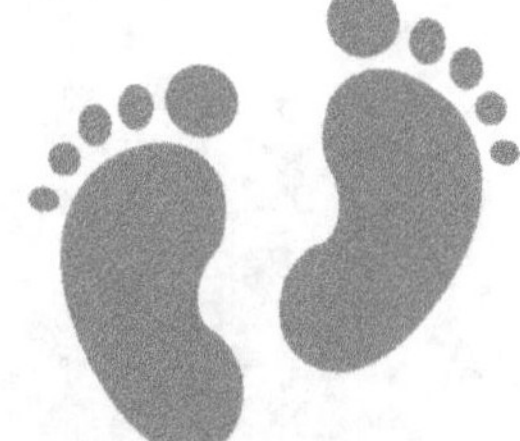

Name

Relationship to the parents/baby

Wishes for the parents

Wishes for the baby

My best advice for parents

Name

Relationship to the parents/baby

Wishes for the parents

Wishes for the baby

My best advice for parents

Name

Relationship to the parents/baby
Wishes for the parents

Wishes for the baby

My best advice for parents

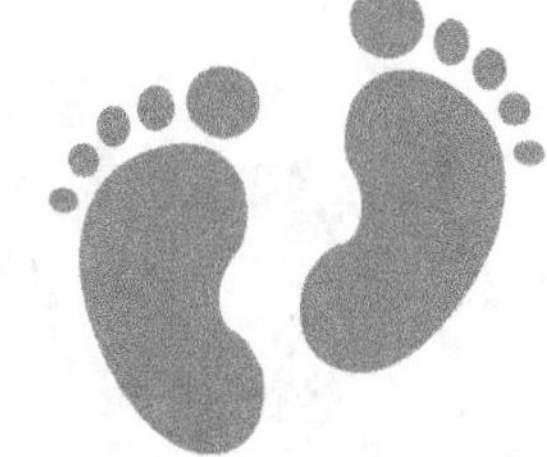

Name

Relationship to the parents/baby

Wishes for the parents

Wishes for the baby

My best advice for parents

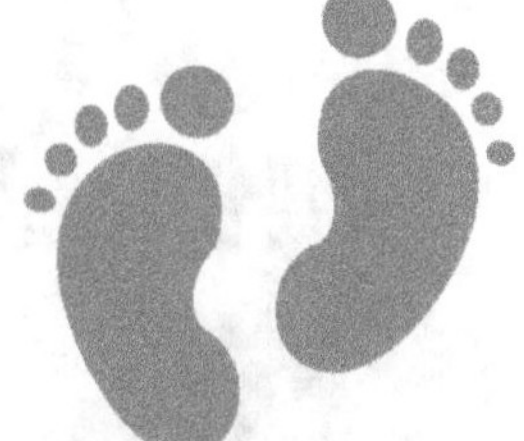

Name

Relationship to the parents/baby

Wishes for the parents

Wishes for the baby

My best advice for parents

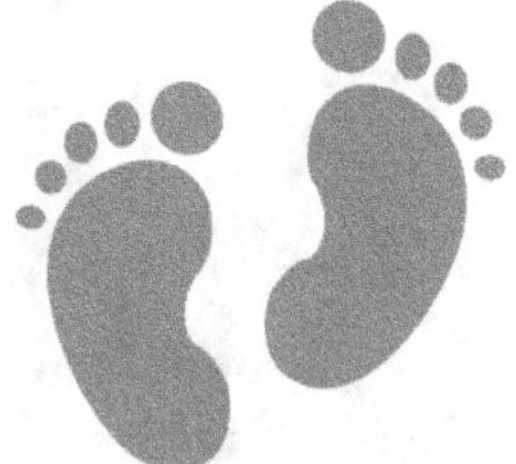

Name

Relationship to the parents/baby

Wishes for the parents

Wishes for the baby

My best advice for parents

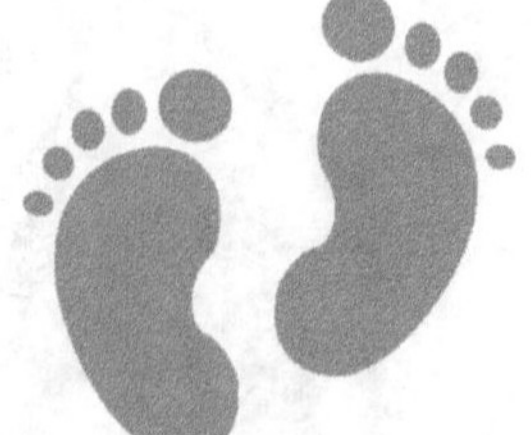

Name

Relationship to the parents/baby

Wishes for the parents

Wishes for the baby

My best advice for parents

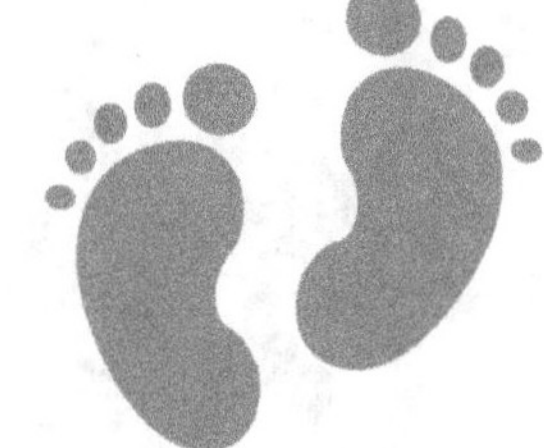

Name

Relationship to the parents/baby

Wishes for the parents

Wishes for the baby

My best advice for parents

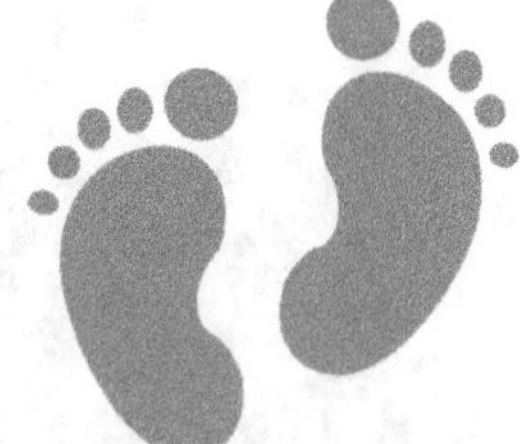

Name

Relationship to the parents/baby

Wishes for the parents

Wishes for the baby

My best advice for parents

Name

Relationship to the parents/baby

Wishes for the parents

Wishes for the baby

My best advice for parents

Name

Relationship to the parents/baby
Wishes for the parents

Wishes for the baby

My best advice for parents

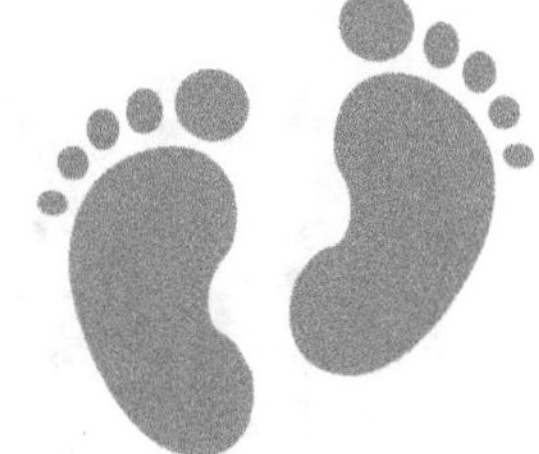

Name

Relationship to the parents/baby

Wishes for the parents

Wishes for the baby

My best advice for parents

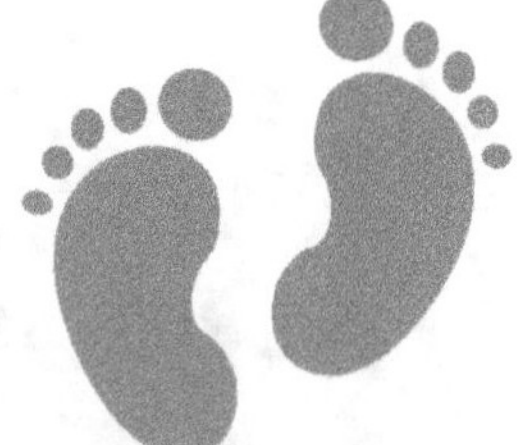

Name

Relationship to the parents/baby

Wishes for the parents

Wishes for the baby

My best advice for parents

Name

Relationship to the parents/baby

Wishes for the parents

Wishes for the baby

My best advice for parents

Name

Relationship to the parents/baby

Wishes for the parents

Wishes for the baby

My best advice for parents

Name

Relationship to the parents/baby

Wishes for the parents

Wishes for the baby

My best advice for parents

Name

Relationship to the parents/baby

Wishes for the parents

Wishes for the baby

My best advice for parents

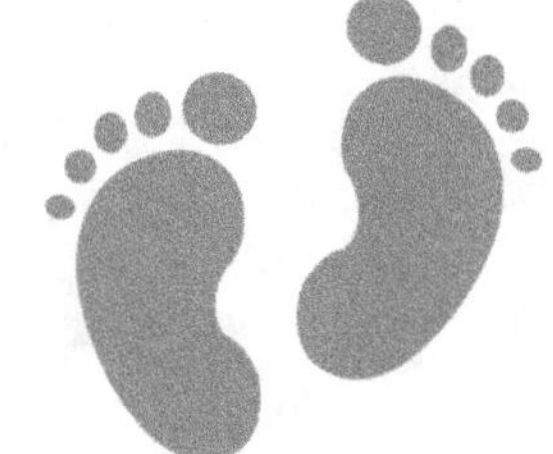

Name

Relationship to the parents/baby

Wishes for the parents

Wishes for the baby

My best advice for parents

Name

Relationship to the parents/baby

Wishes for the parents

Wishes for the baby

My best advice for parents

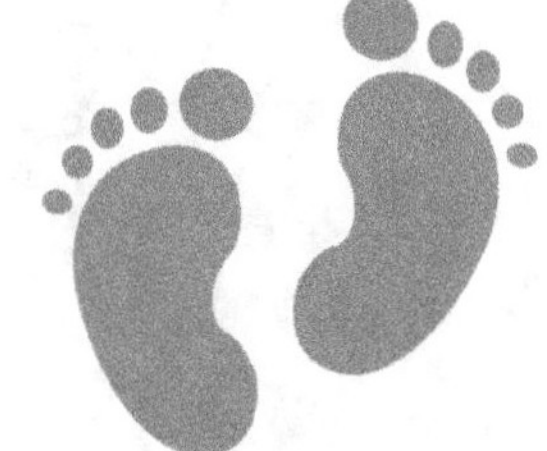

Name

Relationship to the parents/baby

Wishes for the parents

Wishes for the baby

My best advice for parents

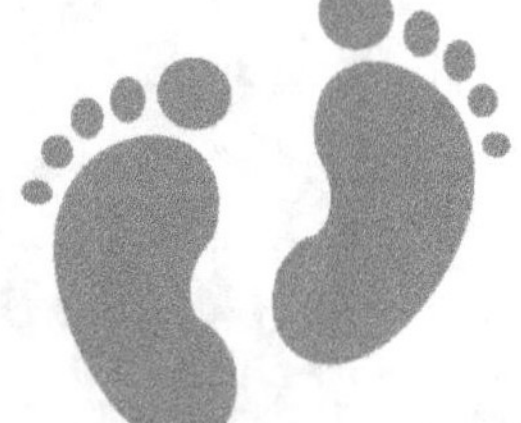

Name

Relationship to the parents/baby

Wishes for the parents

Wishes for the baby

My best advice for parents

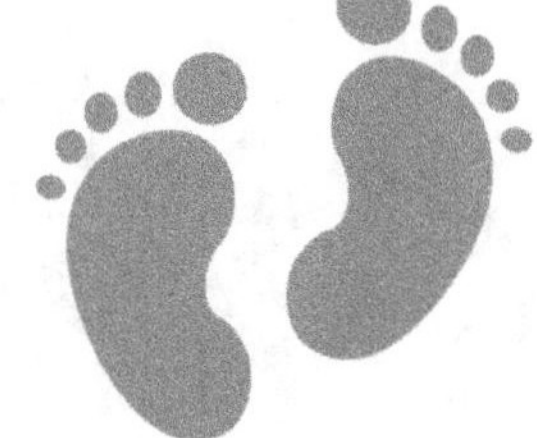

Name

Relationship to the parents/baby

Wishes for the parents

Wishes for the baby

My best advice for parents

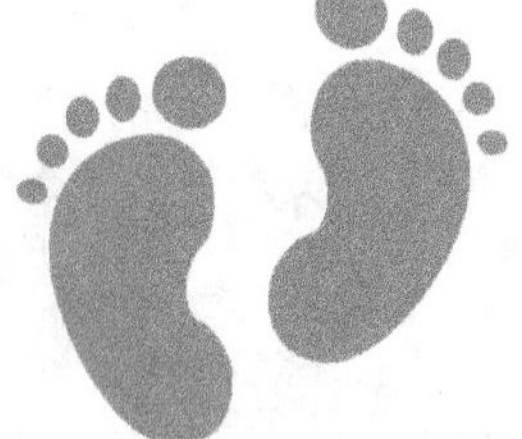

Name

Relationship to the parents/baby

Wishes for the parents

Wishes for the baby

My best advice for parents

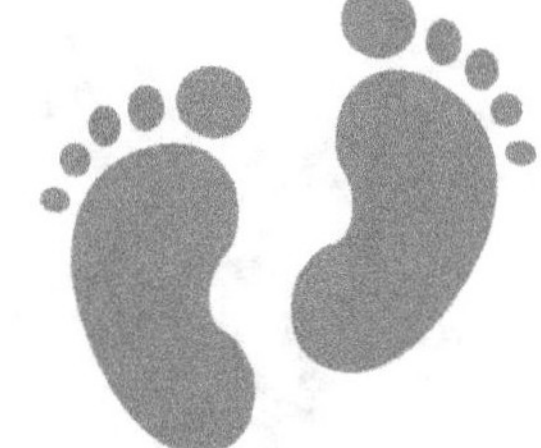

Name

Relationship to the parents/baby

Wishes for the parents

Wishes for the baby

My best advice for parents

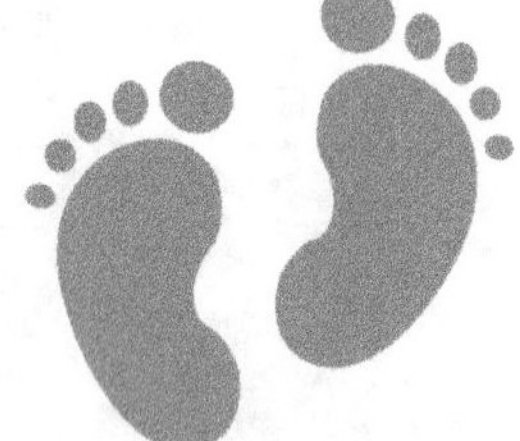

Name

Relationship to the parents/baby

Wishes for the parents

Wishes for the baby

My best advice for parents

Name

Relationship to the parents/baby

Wishes for the parents

Wishes for the baby

My best advice for parents

Name

Relationship to the parents/baby
Wishes for the parents

Wishes for the baby

My best advice for parents

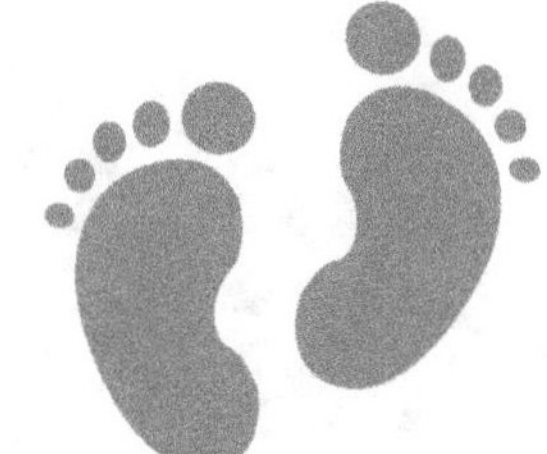

Name

Relationship to the parents/baby

Wishes for the parents

Wishes for the baby

My best advice for parents

Name

Relationship to the parents/baby

Wishes for the parents

Wishes for the baby

My best advice for parents

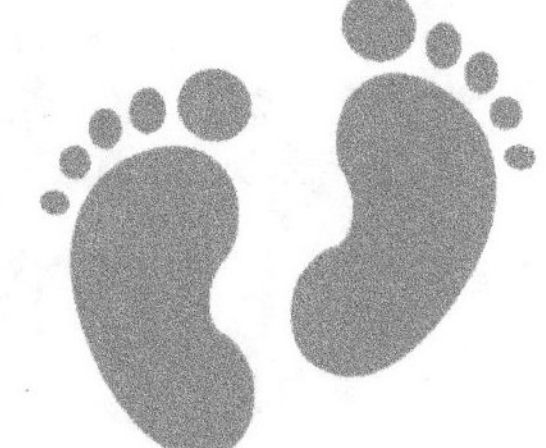

Name

Relationship to the parents/baby

Wishes for the parents

Wishes for the baby

My best advice for parents

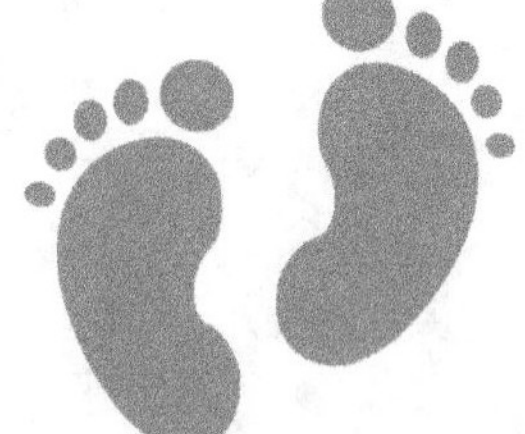

Name

Relationship to the parents/baby

Wishes for the parents

Wishes for the baby

My best advice for parents

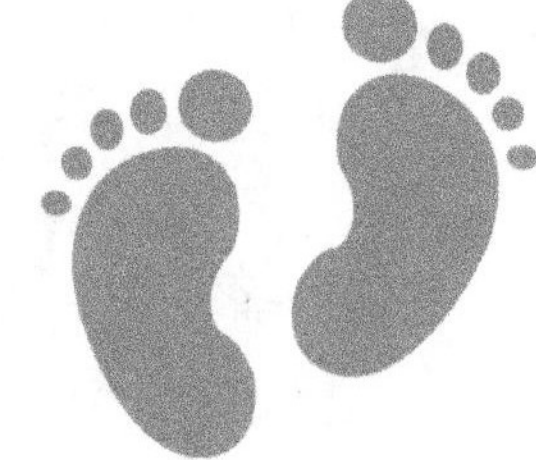

Name

Relationship to the parents/baby

Wishes for the parents

Wishes for the baby

My best advice for parents

Name

Relationship to the parents/baby
Wishes for the parents

Wishes for the baby

My best advice for parents

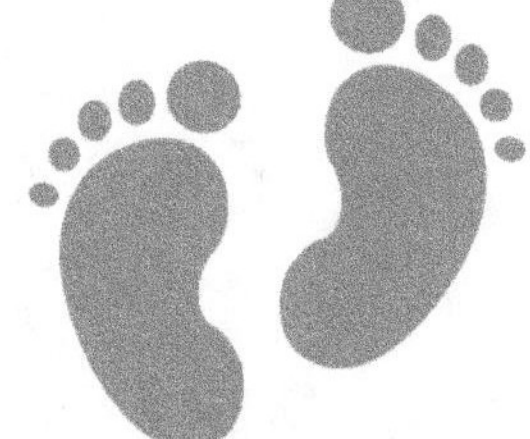

Name

Relationship to the parents/baby

Wishes for the parents

Wishes for the baby

My best advice for parents

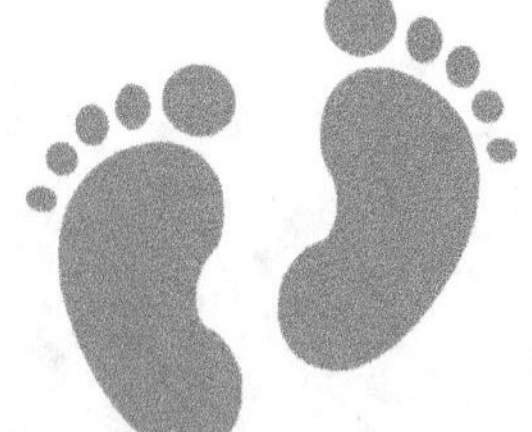

Name

Relationship to the parents/baby

Wishes for the parents

Wishes for the baby

My best advice for parents

Name

Relationship to the parents/baby
Wishes for the parents

Wishes for the baby

My best advice for parents

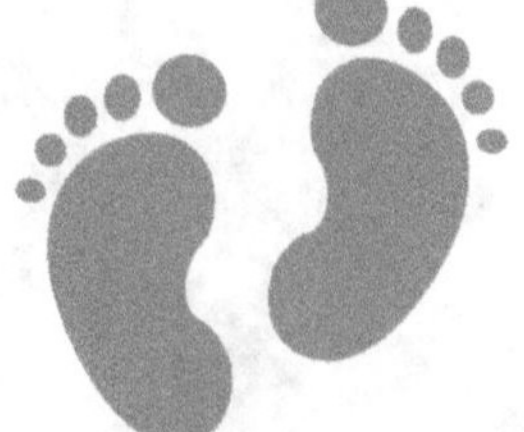

Thank you
We hope you enjoyed our book

For us, your feedback is very important
Please let us know how you liked our book at:

oliviabrooks2222@gmail.com

Hope to see you again